THIS BOOK BELONGS TO:

Belle journals

CONNECT WITH US AT:
BELLEJOURNALS.COM
FACEBOOK.COM/BELLEJOURNALS
INSTAGRAM.COM/BELLEJOURNALS
PINTEREST.COM/BELLEJOURNALS
TWITTER.COM/BELLEJOURNALS

FIND YOUR NEXT JOURNAL AT:
WWW.AMAZON.COM/AUTHOR/BELLEJOURNALS

67242451R00083

Made in the USA
Columbia, SC
24 July 2019